WHAT MAKES A LEONARDO
A LEONARDO?

Richard Mühlberger

WITHDRAWN

The Metropolitan Museum of Art
Viking

NEW YORK

VIKING

First published in 1994 by The Metropolitan Museum of Art, New York, and Viking, a division of Penguin Books USA Inc., 375 Hudson Street, New York, New York 10014, U.S.A. and Penguin Books Canada Ltd., 10 Alcorn Avenue, Toronto, Ontario, Canada M4V 3B2.

Produced by the Department of Special Publications, The Metropolitan Museum of Art
Series Editor: Mary Beth Brewer
Production: Elizabeth Stoneman
Front Cover Design: Marleen Adlerblum
Design: Nai Y. Chang
Printing and Binding: A. Mondadori, Verona, Italy

Library of Congress Cataloging-in-Publication Data
Mühlberger, Richard. What makes a Leonardo a Leonardo?/Richard Mühlberger. p. cm.
ISBN 0-670-85744-0 (Viking)
ISBN 087099-724-6 (MMA)
1. Leonardo, da Vinci, 1452–1519—Criticism and interpretation—Juvenile literature. 2. Painting, Italian—Juvenile literature. 3. Painting, Renaissance—Italy—Juvenile literature. [1. Leonardo, da Vinci, 1452–1519. 2. Painting, Italian. 3. Art appreciation.] I. Title.
ND623.L5M73 1994 759.5—dc20 94-18106 CIP AC

10 9 8 7 6 5 4 3 2 1

ILLUSTRATIONS

Unless otherwise noted, all works are by Leonardo da Vinci and are paintings on panel.

Pages 1 and 2: *Mona Lisa*, 30³/₈ x 20⁷/₈ in., Musée du Louvre, Paris, © PHOTO R.M.N.

Page 6: *Self-Portrait* (?), red chalk, 13¹/₈ x 8³/₈ in., Biblioteca Reale, Turin; photograph, Scala/Art Resource, New York.

Page 8: Workshop of Andrea del Verrocchio, *Madonna and Child*, tempera and gold on wood, 26 x 19 in., The Metropolitan Museum of Art, Bequest of Benjamin Altman, 1913, 14.40.647.

Page 9: View of Florence; photograph, Scala/Art Resource, New York.

Page 11: Andrea del Verrocchio and Workshop, *The Baptism of Christ*, 69⁵/₈ x 59¹/₂ in., Galleria degli Uffizi, Florence; photograph, Scala/Art Resource, New York.

Page 14: *The Annunciation*, 41 x 85³/₈ in., Galleria degli Uffizi, Florence; photograph, Scala/Art Resource, New York.

Page 16: *Ginevra de' Benci* (reverse), 15 x 14¹/₂ in., Ailsa Mellon Bruce Fund, © 1994 Board of Trustees, National Gallery of Art, Washington.

Page 17: *Ginevra de' Benci* (obverse), 15¹/₄ x 14¹/₂ in., Ailsa Mellon Bruce Fund, © 1994 Board of Trustees, National Gallery of Art, Washington; photograph, Jose A. Naranjo.

Page 19: *The Adoration of the Magi*, 96⁷/₈ x 95⁵/₈ in., Galleria degli Uffizi, Florence; photograph, Erich Lessing/Art Resource, New York.

Page 20: Sandro Botticelli, *The Adoration of the Magi*, 43³/₄ x 52³/₄ in., Galleria degli Uffizi, Florence; photograph, Scala/Art Resource, New York.

Page 22: *Lady with an Ermine (Cecilia Gallerani)*, 21¹/₄ x 15³/₈ in., Czartoryski Museum, Cracow; photograph, Scala/Art Resource, New York.

Page 24: *A Bear Walking*, metalpoint on light buff prepared paper, 4¹/₁₆ x 5¹/₄ in., The Metropolitan Museum of Art, Robert Lehman Collection, 1975, 1975.1.369.

Page 24: *Allegorical Design*, pen and brown ink, 7¹⁵/₁₆ x 5³/₈ in., The Metropolitan Museum of Art, Rogers Fund, 1917, 17.142.2 (recto).

Page 25: *Study for the Sforza Monument*, metalpoint on paper coated with a blue-colored preparation, 6 x 7³/₈ in., Royal Library, Windsor Castle (RL 12358), The Royal Collection © Her Majesty Queen Elizabeth II.

Page 27: *The Virgin of the Rocks*, 78 x 48³/₈ in., Musée du Louvre, Paris, © PHOTO R.M.N.

Page 29: *The Star of Bethlehem and Other Plants*, red chalk, pen, and ink, 7³/₄ x 6¹/₄ in., Royal Library, Windsor Castle (RL 12424), The Royal Collection © Her Majesty Queen Elizabeth II.

Page 30: *The Last Supper*, fresco, approx. 181 x 346 in., Santa Maria delle Grazie (refectory), Milan; photograph, Scala/Art Resource, New York.

Page 35: Domenico Ghirlandaio, *The Last Supper*, fresco, approx. 319 in. wide, Ognissanti (refectory), Florence; photograph, Scala/Art Resource, New York.

Page 36: *The Virgin and Child with Saints Anne and John the Baptist*, chalk on paper, 55³/₄ x 41 in., Reproduced by courtesy of the Trustees, The National Gallery, London.

Page 38: Peter Paul Rubens, *The Battle of Anghiari* (copy after Leonardo), pen and ink, pencil and gouache, 17³/₄ x 25¹/₄ in., Cabinet des Dessins, Musée du Louvre, Paris, © PHOTO R.M.N.

Page 41: *Mona Lisa*, 30³/₈ x 20⁷/₈ in., Musée du Louvre, Paris, © PHOTO R.M.N.

Page 42: *The Virgin and Child with Saint Anne*, 66¹/₈ x 44¹/₈ in., Musée du Louvre, Paris, © PHOTO R.M.N.

Page 45: *Saint John the Baptist*, 27¹/₈ x 22³/₈ in., Musée du Louvre, Paris, © PHOTO R.M.N.

Page 46: *A Deluge*, black chalk, pen and ink, 6³/₈ x 8 in., Royal Library, Windsor Castle (RL 12380), The Royal Collection © Her Majesty Queen Elizabeth II.

Page 47: *Studies for a Nativity*, pen and brown ink over metalpoint on pink prepared paper, 7⁵/₈ x 6³/₈ in., The Metropolitan Museum of Art, Rogers Fund, 1917, 17.142.1.

Page 49: *The Virgin of the Rocks*, 74⁵/₈ x 47¹/₄ in., Reproduced by courtesy of the Trustees, The National Gallery, London.

CONTENTS

SELF-PORTRAIT

Meet Leonardo da Vinci

Today Leonardo da Vinci's name is linked to his most famous works, *The Last Supper* and *Mona Lisa*. People who know these paintings usually discover other works by this revolutionary Renaissance master. Though few, his works provide stimulation for the mind as well as the eye, and his many drawings are proof of his genius. We know that Leonardo was famous in his own lifetime, for his talents were mentioned by his contemporaries. The first biography of the artist dates from 1518, the year before his death, and a second one followed about a decade later; both of them are brief. A full biography of Leonardo da Vinci was published in 1550 and again in 1568 by the artist and historian Giorgio Vasari. Vasari compiled legends and facts about many artists in his great book *Lives of the Artists*, which is still used by scholars today. His chapter on Leonardo draws on the stories that were told in the workshops of Florence where Vasari himself had studied art. He also interviewed Leonardo's students and his closest friends.

Leonardo's contemporaries praised the artist's physical beauty and strength. They said that he was charming and generous. All commented favorably on his musical ability, for he sang and played the lyre very well, and they also said that he was an inventor of astounding genius. About his paintings, there was hesitation. According to Vasari, it was hard for Leonardo to be satisfied with his work, so he left more unfinished than he completed. Still, Vasari called him a divinely inspired painter.

As his grandfather Antonio proudly reported, Leonardo was born at 10:30 P.M. on Saturday, April 15, 1452. Antonio lived in Vinci, a village in the beautiful countryside of Tuscany in central Italy. ("Da Vinci" means "from Vinci.") There he looked after a modest old estate.

Leonardo's father, Piero, and his mother, Caterina, did not marry each other. Caterina cared for the infant for a while, then married a local man and raised a family with him. Piero married a woman from Florence, the capital of the region, where generations of his family had found success in their work as notaries, or law clerks. The couple lived there, returning to Vinci occasionally. According to a tax record,

Workshop of Andrea del Verrocchio
MADONNA AND CHILD

Verrocchio was one of the most sophisticated Florentine artists in the fifteenth century and was head of a productive workshop. Pictures of the Madonna and Child were in great demand. The master may have provided the design for this work, and various assistants then painted it.

Leonardo was living with his grandparents when he was five years old. His uncle Francesco was fond of the boy and probably taught him about nature during excursions through the wild countryside that surrounds Vinci. When Francesco died, some fifty years later, he willed his estate to Leonardo, as though he had been his son.

When Leonardo was a teenager, his father brought him to Florence to live. Before the modern unification of Italy, Florence, like other Italian cities of the time, was an independent city-state, with its own government, traditions, and styles of art and architecture. By modern standards, Florence was small, but its power was in its wealth, for many Florentine banks financed wars and governments throughout Europe. During the fifteenth century, the city's achievements in art and architecture astounded all of Europe.

Apprenticeship

When Leonardo arrived in Florence, one of the city's leading artists was Andrea del Verrocchio. Trained as a goldsmith, he was also a painter and sculptor. Leonardo's father knew Verrocchio, and by 1469, Leonardo had become one of his many apprentices.

In Leonardo's day, the apprenticeship system provided all artistic training. Regulated and supervised by guilds that had existed since the Middle Ages, it enabled young men to learn everything from grinding pigments and making brushes to painting altarpieces and carving sculptures. An apprenticeship typically lasted thirteen years—about the length of time that Leonardo served Verrocchio. While in an artist's workshop, an apprentice would advance to journeyman, which qualified him to work at many tasks without supervision, and then to master craftsman (maestro). As a master, Leonardo was expected to imitate perfectly Verrocchio's work, for everything produced in the shop was sold under Verrocchio's name.

Soon after Leonardo began his apprenticeship, Verrocchio made a two-ton gilded ball with a cross on top of it to crown the dome of the city's cathedral. The dome, then the largest in Europe, was the pride of Florence. The crafting of the golden sphere tested Verrocchio's knowledge of metallurgy, sculpture, geometry, casting, engineering, and architecture. Leonardo learned that mastering many skills was one of the goals of an artist. He saw that science and art were inseparable, and became a master of both.

Inventing Renaissance Painting
Florentine achievements in art and architecture put Florence in the forefront of Italian cities and made it the birthplace of the Renaissance, which means "rebirth." Florentines looked anew to the wisdom of the ancient Greeks and Romans, and they strove to rival and even surpass their achievements. For his part in all this creative activity, Leonardo invented a new style of Renaissance painting that was grander and much more lifelike than anything the world had ever seen.

This book looks closely at twelve of Leonardo's paintings. Two of them are unfinished, one is in ruins, and one is lost, known only from copies by other artists! If his paintings present an incomplete picture of Leonardo, his notes and drawings will show the biologist, botanist, engineer, and inventor. There will always be more to Leonardo than eyes can see.

Leonardo was about eighteen years old and had served two years of his apprenticeship when he was asked to complete one of his master's works by painting in an angel.

View of Florence

9

The Baptism of Christ

Verrocchio designed *The Baptism of Christ* with the Renaissance ideal of balance in mind. The artist placed Christ near the middle of the painting. He wears a striped cloth. His hands are folded in prayer, and his head is bowed. Saint John solemnly strides into the shallow Jordan River to baptize his cousin. His sinewy limbs, strongly sculpted face, and energetic stance are sharply defined. To balance his figure, Verrocchio placed two kneeling angels and a tall palm tree on the left.

Verrocchio included several symbols in his painting that would be familiar to his contemporaries. Above Christ appears "the Spirit of God descending like a dove" that is described in the biblical account of the baptism of Jesus. Above the dove, a pair of hands represents God the Father, who announced at this event that Jesus "is my beloved Son, in whom I am well pleased." Jesus, the Holy Spirit, and God the Father appear in a line down the middle, connecting the three parts of the Christian Trinity. John the Baptist's staff is topped with a cross, a reminder of Christ's eventual death. The narrow banner that spirals from the Baptist's hand bears the Latin words *Ecce Agnus*, the beginning of "Behold the Lamb of God," words John spoke as Jesus approached him to be baptized. Lambs were used for temple sacrifices in biblical times, so the expression "Lamb of God" symbolizes the sacrifice of Jesus on the cross.

Surpassing His Master

Leonardo painted a small and important part of the work, the angel on the left. Verrocchio painted the second angel, but Leonardo surpassed his master. In fact, Vasari said that Verrocchio gave up painting because he could not render an angel as beautifully as his apprentice could.

The legs of Leonardo's kneeling angel, like the feet of John, point toward Jesus. The angel

looks at Jesus in adoration as he holds his golden cloak, which hangs across his forearms and down to the rocky earth. One tuft of grass grows where its golden lining meets the blue folds of the angel's gown. Everything is in harmony, in the precise and crisp fashion that Verrocchio demanded. Only the face of Leonardo's angel shows softness.

One reason for this difference lies in the two artists' techniques. Verrocchio's painting was done with tempera, a durable paint made with egg yolks that had been widely used in Europe since about the year 1200. Leonardo preferred to mix tempera with oil paint, which was still a novelty in Italy. Its colors were richer and more luminous than those of tempera. The misty landscape behind the angels was first painted with tempera, then lightly covered in oil paint. Leonardo's love of nature is evident in background landscapes in many of his paintings. Like the landscape behind the angels, they lose their colors to an overall blue tone. Veils of moisture and golden light soften details.

In 1472, Leonardo was accepted as a master craftsman by the Company of Saint Luke, the painters' guild. Although he could have gone off on his own, he decided to continue as Verrocchio's assistant.

The Annunciation

This painting was for many years displayed in the church of the convent of Monte Oliveto outside Florence. Because no historian, including Vasari, ever mentioned it, much time passed before it was recognized as a work by Leonardo. In it, the angel Gabriel, just descended from heaven, kneels formally on the left. "Fear not," he says, as he explains to the woman opposite him that she will "bring forth . . . the Son of God." The woman, Mary, is startled at the news. She accepts the announcement by pledging that she is "the handmaid of the Lord. Be it unto me according to thy word." The angel's gesture is one of blessing, and Mary's is one of acceptance.

This very important Christian scene was frequently painted during the Renaissance. Here Leonardo created a wide, narrow painting with the sacred figures presented traditionally. In the distance, between the holy figures, dark trees and a faint mountain point up toward heaven. The gap in the row of trees allows a view into the vast distance.

Behind Gabriel and Mary, a wide, low wall encloses a garden, a symbol of Mary's virginity. She sits in front of her house, framed by its large cornerstones, which refer to her role as a foundation of the Church. The carved marble lectern in front of the Virgin might have reminded some viewers of a casket and the eventual death of the child to be born. Its intricate carving of lush leaves and a garland is in the style of Verrocchio's sculpture. On it is a prayer book. Mary's fingers elegantly mark a passage in it.

A technique to indicate distance, called aerial or atmospheric perspective, makes the background look far from the figures up front. Everything in the foreground is sharply defined and colorful, but the harbor and the mountains beyond it take on the color of the sky. This blurs details, makes them hazy, and masks their true colors. When background features are painted lighter, they seem farther away. Leonardo knew that it was not just the actual colors that made them look the way they do. Light and distance change the appearance of everything. Capturing the effects of light was one of Leonardo's goals.

Verrocchio's shop had a fine reputation for solid craftsmanship and design, so Leonardo had to follow his master's ideas. He also had to help teach the art of painting to younger assistants and apprentices. It is likely that he assigned parts of the painting to them, but he saved the most important parts for himself.

In addition to his work as a painter, Leonardo received other varied assignments from Verrocchio. He was asked to design settings for military spectacles called jousts. The staging of entertainments for the Duke of Milan's visit to Florence in 1471 also fell to him. There is no doubt that all of Leonardo's costumes and sets were splendid, but they were meant to delight only for a day. Nothing exists of them today.

The lush garden at Gabriel's feet seems to respond to his message, as the varied plants writhe and surge. Even this early in his career, Leonardo carefully observed the movement found in nature.

Ginevra de' Benci

In the portrait of Ginevra de' Benci, Leonardo flooded light on her hair, face, and shoulders. It causes the top of her head to glow and reveals rivulets of tiny curls that part in the shape of a triangle. It illuminates the smooth curve of her lofty forehead and the crescents of her eyelids, while emphasizing the height of her cheeks and the roundness of her chin. Below her long neck, made strong by shadows, light reveals a sheer blouse under the squared bodice of the dress. She is modest, aristocratic, and perhaps a little sullen. Her eyes seem narrowed in thought.

Leonardo once advised artists to place a light figure against a dark background in order to make it look three dimensional. He followed his own advice and painted a dark bush behind Ginevra's head. It has a jagged form, and she seems to emerge from it. The spiky shrub is a juniper bush, called *ginepro* in Italian. Since the word sounds like the woman's name, it serves as her emblem. Hundreds of small needles become uneven linear patterns against the sky, and the ones

behind Ginevra's right shoulder crisscross like the web of a spider. Below, to the right, water flickers with the reflections of other foliage.

The back of the wood panel on which Leonardo painted Ginevra's portrait is also painted and conveys a message about the young woman. It shows a palm branch and a laurel branch, both used in ancient times for wreaths of honor. Between them is a juniper twig. All three are entwined with a narrow scroll bearing the Latin phrase *Virtutem forma decorat* ("Beauty is the ornament of Virtue"). The lower part of the branches is missing, because about one-third of the painting has been cut off, as well as parts of the sides. It may be that Ginevra de' Benci's hands were originally included in Leonardo's painting.

Ginevra married in 1474 at the age of seventeen, and Leonardo's painting probably was prepared to celebrate that event. With its juniper bush and Latin slogan, it is a kind of poem about the young woman's name, beauty, and virtue.

The Adoration of the Magi

Leonardo lived in Verrocchio's house until he was almost thirty years of age. By 1479, he had his own lodgings, and two years later he began a painting that was more radical and expressive than anything seen before.

Abundance and Variety

At the center of Leonardo's unfinished masterpiece is the head of the Virgin Mary. Turned to watch the Christ Child on her lap, she does not acknowledge the strange pageant around her.

Bearded old men keep their distance, three of them Magi bearing gifts. Other spectators are packed close to one another. Young and old, each one different, their faces and gestures form a gallery of questioning and wondering expressions. For storytelling paintings like this one, Leonardo thought that "abundance and variety" were important to make the image lifelike. He told artists to avoid repetition in favor of "a mixture of men of various appearances, of different ages, and costumes, also mixed with women, children, dogs, horses, buildings, fields, and hills." *The Adoration of the Magi* shows just the kind of variety Leonardo described.

A carob tree crowns the rocky knoll that acts as Mary's throne, and a palm tree rises behind it. Beyond them is a fantastic building, made mysterious by two sets of stairs that go nowhere. A horse rears as it passes under a broken arch, and two others approach the mother and her baby. On the other side of the tree are more horses and riders.

Only shades of brown appear because in keeping with his definition of painting as "a composition of light and shade," Leonardo painted the shadows first. He would have applied colors on top of them to make his objects look three-dimensional. What seems at first to be drawing was painted with brushes, as was the

shading. Canvas was not yet used for painting, so carpenters prepared planks of hardwood, smoothing them and joining them snugly. *The Adoration*, Leonardo's first large painting, is about eight feet high and eight feet wide.

Breaking the Rules

For his unique composition, Leonardo broke many rules of linear perspective, a technique invented in Florence around the beginning of the century. Artists used perspective to make the objects they painted look as if they went back into space, as if the picture frame were a window. One of the rules of linear perspective was that the artist should have a single viewing point. But here, we look at the Virgin and Child in the foreground from above, as her lap is clearly visible, while we see the background activity from almost straight ahead. Leonardo used two different points of view to make all the action visible. Another rule of linear perspective is that all objects must be made smaller as they move farther into the background. But Leonardo did not follow this rule closely. The Virgin is much bigger than the men who surround her. The figures around the strange building are as tall as the arches! Leonardo made the scene look convincing, even though he broke the rules.

Many versions of the Adoration were produced in Florence during Leonardo's lifetime. Usually they were very formal and orderly. Sandro Botticelli, one of the most famous artists of the day, had worked in Verrocchio's workshop, where he had become friendly with Leonardo. Botticelli's *Adoration* was done a few years before Leonardo's. The two works are not at all alike.

In Botticelli's work, the composition is calm and balanced, and it follows the rules of linear perspective. His figures are outlined and painted in bright, clear colors. The Magi and their servants are up front, so they stand out from the crowd. The viewer looks up at them, as though watching characters perform on a stage.

In Leonardo's *Adoration*, the figures are not crisply outlined, but made up of deeply shaded areas. The Magi are mixed with all sorts of other characters, forming a swirl of commotion. There is a feeling of genuine wonder and confusion in their faces.

Sandro Botticelli
The Adoration of the Magi

Leonardo's father helped him secure this large and important commission. Among his clients were the friars of a monastery near Florence called San Donato a Scopeto, who wanted a painting for their main altar. Piero da Vinci recommended his talented son. With ten years' experience as a painter and a fine background from his years in Verrocchio's workshop, Leonardo was well qualified for the contract to paint *The Adoration of the Magi*. Unfortunately, the artist abandoned the project to move to another city.

While planning the altarpiece for San Donato a Scopeto, Leonardo made a silver lyre in the shape of a horse's head. Lorenzo de' Medici, the most powerful man in Florence, decided that the musical instrument would make a magnificent gift to Ludovico Sforza, the new ruler of Milan. At the same time, the talents of Leonardo would make an even more impressive gift. So it was arranged that the lyre and its maker would enter the service of Ludovico. In 1482, Leonardo entrusted the unfinished altarpiece to Amerigo Benci, Ginevra's father, and went north to Milan.

Lady with an Ermine

The young woman and the ermine in her arms twist in the same way, each body showing a three-quarter view. Their heads turn in the other direction. Leonardo placed the animal's limp paw near the taut fingers of the woman. She holds the wild pet with a light touch that seems to soothe the animal.

The woman is dressed fashionably. Her hair is engulfed in gauze, her forehead entwined with ribbon, and her neck elegantly circled by black beads. The tight headdress contrasts with the billowing sleeves of her dress. She smiles contentedly, seemingly pleased with a happy thought passing through her mind.

Daylight falls on the woman's face and shoulders. Leonardo placed her against a dark backdrop to make her appear to emerge from it. It also emphasizes the pale beauty of her skin, the flawless fur of the animal, and the gentle curves of her head, cheek, and shoulder. The long belly of the small beast forms a similar curve.

Nature is Jealous

Contemporaries of Leonardo mentioned that he painted a portrait of a young lady named Cecilia Gallerani. The poet Bernardo Bellincioni, who served the Milanese duke, wrote of this portrait, "Nature herself is jealous, since the beautiful young woman is so lifelike that she seems to be listening and only lacks speech." The subject was a close friend of Ludovico Sforza, and was the most powerful woman in his court. The pure white ermine symbolized her loyalty to him. Like the juniper in the portrait of Ginevra de' Benci, the animal is a pun on the lady's name. Gallerani sounds like the Greek word for ermine.

Leonardo was in Milan in the service of the duke for more than a dozen years. The artist wrote to introduce himself to the ruler in about 1482, describing his ability to build bridges, drain

A BEAR WALKING

To understand an animal's character, Leonardo studied the way it moved. In his notes he wrote, "Here is to be depicted the foot of the bear or ape or other animals to show how they vary from the foot of man, or, say, the feet of certain birds."

him the money to complete it. For sixteen years, the artist labored on the monument whenever he could. In the end, a twenty-six-foot-high clay model of it was completed.

ALLEGORICAL DESIGN
This drawing shows Leonardo's distinctive handwriting. He was left-handed, and he wrote from right to left.

ditches, design and supply armaments of all kinds, and "contrive various and endless means of offense and defense" in warfare. Near the close of his letter, he presented his credentials as an architect, then said, in an almost offhand way, "I can carry out sculpture in marble, bronze, or clay, and also I can do in painting whatever may be done." Leonardo's ability in bronze sculpture probably appealed to the duke most, for he wanted to erect a grand bronze monument to his famous father, showing him mounted on a horse.

The ambitious project was always on Leonardo's mind, but Ludovico was slow to give

STUDY FOR THE SFORZA MONUMENT

A rearing equestrian monument had never been done before, because it was too difficult to balance its weight, but Leonardo welcomed the challenge. Here he considered using the figure of a fallen enemy to support the horse's forelegs. The statue was never cast because the duke used the bronze intended for it to make weapons instead.

The Virgin of the Rocks

A dark, craggy grotto shelters a woman, two children, and an angel. The window that opens through rocks to the background shows that the grotto is one of many outcroppings on the edge of a winding river. The clusters of rock formations in the background support little life, but plants abound near the four figures. Leonardo describes all of the rocks and the lush plants that spring from them in great detail, while the background landscape is misty and muted.

The Virgin Mary is kneeling in the grotto. The traditional color of her cloak is blue, but Leonardo lined it in gold to make it richer, like a garment a queen might wear. A bold swag of the fine fabric crosses her waist, puckering into angular peaks like the blue folds at her knees. Her simple cape is cinched at the neck by a dark, polished stone surrounded by pearls.

John the Baptist kneels on the left, protected by Mary's embracing touch. Opposite him is Jesus, Mary's son and John's cousin. The children face each other, John in a worshiping pose, and Jesus with his hand raised in blessing. Tradition says that the sweet and melancholy angel is Uriel. Mary rewards her son with a blessing. Her hovering hand is above the angel's hand, which points to the Baptist. The angel looks directly out, instructing viewers to honor Christ as little Saint John does. Leonardo carefully arranged all the hands to focus on the figure of Jesus.

Artists often showed Jesus blessing his cousin with two upraised fingers. By Leonardo's time, paintings with the Virgin Mary and the two holy children were familiar and dear to Italians. Leonardo did not drastically alter this beloved format, but he made one important change: He removed Jesus from Mary's lap, making him independent. Saint Luke reported that John lived in

the desert, preparing himself for his work as a preacher who announced the coming of Jesus. In *The Virgin of the Rocks*, Leonardo showed John receiving his commission from Jesus.

Leonardo lived in the house of a family of artists named Preda. Ambrogio da Preda, who was known for his portraits, had just been made official painter to the court of Milan. His two brothers were also artists. Leonardo, Ambrogio, and one of the brothers, Evangelista, received a commission in 1483 from a devotional organization called the Confraternity of the Immaculate Conception of the Virgin Mary, which wanted a large altarpiece celebrating the holiness of Mary. The Confraternity wrote a long contract that told Leonardo and the da Preda brothers what to include in the altarpiece. The original plan was to honor Mary with a large painted panel in the center flanked by smaller ones and surrounded by a large sculpted and painted wooden frame. The central panel, painted by Leonardo, was supposed to show the Virgin and Child surrounded by angels and two prophets, but the artist chose to tell the story of Jesus and Saint John as babies instead. Today, Leonardo's painting is preserved in the Louvre in Paris, one of the greatest museums in the world. Leonardo made a second version of the painting, and later his followers painted their own interpretations of the great work of art.

In the three years that the artist had been in Milan, he had designed costumes and settings for court weddings and tournaments and had painted a portrait. He also had built a model for Milan's cathedral, which had been in construction for many years. He worked on the great horse on his own, for it was not yet an official commission, and he earned nothing for his advice on military matters. In the meantime, he sought commissions outside the court. The altarpiece for the Confraternity was one of them. In 1495, the duke finally gave Leonardo an exciting new commission. Ludovico was helping the monks of Santa Maria delle Grazie in Milan to modernize and expand their church and monastery. The refectory, or dining room, had just been enlarged, and Leonardo was asked to paint a mural of the Last Supper, a scene that traditionally adorned refectories. The grand result, almost thirty feet wide and fourteen feet high, quickly became the most celebrated painting of its day.

THE STAR OF BETHLEHEM AND OTHER PLANTS

Leonardo made drawings to record his observations of nature. Their beauty and sensitivity make them works of art as well as scientific studies.

The Last Supper

Jesus is sorrowful, his eyes cast downward. An open door frames his head, isolating him from his twelve disciples. The erect posture, tilted head, and extended arms form a triangle. His hands summarize the sacred act he is performing. They lightly brush the white linen cloth that covers the table in front of him. His right hand reaches for a glass of wine. His left hand, palm up, gestures toward the unleavened bread that he will bless, break, and share with his disciples. The words that he is about to utter will transform the last Passover celebration of Jesus and his followers into the first Christian church service. He called the bread "my body" and the wine "my blood," and instructed his followers to partake of it "in remembrance of me."

Leonardo arranged the disciples in groups of three, six men on either side of Jesus, all reacting to the mysterious words of their Master, as they question a prophecy he had made at the start of the dinner. "One of you shall betray me," Jesus said. Leonardo followed the Evangelist

Luke's account of the disciples' response to their Master's startling words: "They began to inquire among themselves, which of them it was that should do this thing. And there was also a strife among them, which of them should be accounted the greatest."

Is It I?

Within each group, men lean and gesture toward Jesus, while others sway away from him. The movement of hands, arms, and bodies creates a rhythm of crashing waves of emotion. Leonardo wrote that "the good painter has essentially two things to represent: a person and that person's state of mind. The first is easy, the second difficult, for one has to achieve it through the

face to the left of Jesus. Judas clutches a money pouch with one hand while his other hovers over a dish, a reference to Jesus's claim that "he that dippeth his hand with me into the dish, he shall betray me." In February 1498, a contemporary wrote, "It is impossible to imagine the apostles more alive and attentive to the voice of ineffable truth . . . . Each one of them seems to react with word and gesture."

Jesus's announcement of his betrayal was a shocking moment during the Last Supper. The spiritual high point was the blessing of bread and wine, a ceremony that has been repeated daily for almost two thousand years in Christian churches. Other artists selected one or the other episode to portray, but not both. The betrayal called for deeply human reactions, while the blessing required a feeling of inward peace. Leonardo was the first artist to focus on both. Because they happened at different times during the supper, he decided to portray a moment in between.

Jesus Is the Center

Jesus is the physical and spiritual center of his table. Leonardo also wanted him to command the large room in which the mural was painted. To do this, he extended the ceiling lines of the monks' refectory into the painted room of *The Last Supper*. Diagonal lines mark the meeting of the wall and ceiling, as well as the tops of the wall hangings. If extended, the lines would come together at the head of Jesus; they are echoed in the angles of his arms. Leonardo also shaded the

gestures and movements of the limbs." One of the disciples points to heaven and another points to himself, asking, "Is it I?", the question repeated in the accounts of the event by Matthew, Mark, and John. Leonardo dramatically describes Judas, the disciple who will betray Jesus, by making him the only one who leans forward on the table. He also obscures Judas's face in shadow—the third left wall more than the right, as if his painted room were illuminated by the sunlight coming from the windows on the refectory's left wall.

What *The Last Supper* was really meant to look like is not known, for it began to decay during Leonardo's own lifetime. Vasari said it was "so badly preserved that one can only see a muddle of blots." Leonardo did not use the traditional, durable technique of fresco painting, in which paint is applied to wet plaster so that the picture becomes part of the wall. The method required precise drawings to be transferred onto the plaster, and the quick application of paint before the plaster dried. Because Leonardo worked slowly and was always revising, he chose to experiment with various techniques on dry, instead of wet, plaster. Unfortunately, his mural started to disintegrate even as he worked on it, and it has been restored many times over the centuries.

Enemy soldiers invaded Milan in October of 1499, forcing the duke to flee. Leonardo had no work in the city, so for five months he traveled through northern Italy, first to Mantua, then to Venice, then back to Florence. It is said that the invaders destroyed his huge model of the horse by using it for target practice. But by now, another great concept was in Leonardo's mind—a painting about the holiness of the Virgin Mary.

Domenico Ghirlandaio
THE LAST SUPPER

The Florentine painter Domenico Ghirlandaio painted this fresco of The Last Supper *about ten years before Leonardo painted his celebrated composition. Leonardo used the same traditional format, but he greatly increased the size of the disciples in relation to the table, and he overlapped them in ways that would be impossible in real life. This increases the emotional impact of the scene.*

The Virgin and Child with Saints Anne and John the Baptist

When Leonardo settled in Florence, he lived in the monastery of Servite monks who asked him to paint an altarpiece for their church. Leonardo made a number of drawings of the Virgin Mary with her mother, son, and John the Baptist. This cartoon, meaning a drawing intended to be transferred to a final work, was probably related to the commission. In it, Leonardo pictured the origin of Mary's holiness. John the Baptist was the patron saint of Florence, and Saint Anne, Mary's mother, was also loved by the Florentine Republic. Therefore, the subject had a patriotic as well as a religious meaning for the city.

Legends say that Anne was very old when Mary was born, but in Leonardo's drawing she and her daughter look like sisters. With their heads close together, they converse about the children at their knees. Mary looks at her son while Anne points a finger straight up. Her hand is unfinished, so it stands out and seems to be floating between the infants.

Holy Union

Mary sits balanced lightly on her mother's right knee. In paintings of the Virgin Mary, her seat was of great symbolic importance: When she sat on the ground, she was known as the Virgin of Humility; a throne made her a queen; and when she sat on clouds, she was the Queen of Heaven. Putting her on her mother's lap was a striking new idea in art. Leonardo's deep shadows and his clever confusion of legs obliterated any separation between them. It showed the union of the two women and the baby Jesus. Anne's emphatic gesture is a reminder that Christ's holiness is from heaven. Leonardo demonstrates that Mary comes from Anne, and that Jesus comes from Mary and God.

Peter Paul Rubens
THE BATTLE OF ANGHIARI
(COPY AFTER LEONARDO)

The Battle of Anghiari

In 1503, the new government of Florence asked Leonardo to paint a patriotic mural on one of the walls of the new Council Chamber of the Palazzo Vecchio, the city hall. He was to portray a battle that took place in 1440 at Anghiari, a village about forty miles southeast of Florence, when the small Republic of Florence triumphed over the powerful army of Milan. *The Battle of Anghiari* was Leonardo's largest and most important mural. Although it is totally lost, it has been remembered for more than four hundred years from descriptions and through copies.

Leonardo was given a huge expanse of wall to paint—probably twenty-four feet high and sixty feet wide —but his concept was even larger. He wanted to demonstrate all of the pain, loss, and emotion of war, which he had described earlier in one of his notebooks. His subject also gave Leonardo a chance to explore further the theme of the Sforza monument, that of a man on horseback.

Leonardo created a swirl of men and horses, dramatizing the battle for the standard, the pole and banner that symbolize the Florentine Republic. The two warriors on the left probably represent the Florentines, who take hold of the standard and fight back the charge of the Milanese on the right. More soldiers are defeated and fall. Leonardo showed the high-pitched emotion of battle: the anger, the struggle, the terror, and the strength of men and horses. These psychological states had never been captured so vividly in art before.

Leonardo and his helpers spent a year and a half preparing a cartoon for the mural. Leonardo began painting on Friday, June 6, 1505, at 9:30 A.M. He wrote, "I was just picking up my brush when the weather took a turn for the worse . . . and the cartoon began to come apart, and water went everywhere." Leonardo made repairs and began painting, but he stopped in May 1506 to return to Milan. As in *The Last Supper*, Leonardo did not use the traditional fresco technique, but experimented. The results were disastrous, as the plaster would not dry and the colors dripped down the wall. Although he never completed this great work, it was admired by all who saw it in its unfinished state.

Michelangelo, a rival, was asked to paint a battle scene across the room from Leonardo's, but he did not complete his mural, either. The works were so astonishing, however, that many artists made copies of both murals. Eventually, Vasari, who was also an artist, painted over them with his own battle scene. The copy of *The Battle of Anghiari* that is thought to capture the original's spirit best is by the great seventeenth-century Flemish artist Peter Paul Rubens.

Mona Lisa

Mona Lisa is the most famous painting in the world. Its composition is straightforward: A woman quietly sits in a chair in front of a landscape, her body forming a strong triangular shape. She is dressed simply. The layers of fine clothing she wears are softly colored, and she is free of jewelry. Her body is turned away from the artist. Leonardo believed that a person's soul shows in the eyes. Mona Lisa's are kind and playful. The meaning of her smile is less obvious. Vasari said that it was divine rather than human, and many have wondered at its significance.

Leonardo's studies of nature made him understand that in real life people, animals, and objects of all sorts do not have outlines. Traditionally, artists outlined figures to separate them from their backgrounds. Leonardo decided to eliminate outlines from his art. He formed *Mona Lisa* of light and shadow. Lines are not drawn between her fingers; shadows separate them. Her nose is painted with gradations of light and dark that blend, or melt, into one another.

Leonardo's technique is called *sfumato*, from the Italian word for smoke, *fumo*. Leonardo himself wrote that his method was "without lines or borders, in the manner of smoke." This new technique makes Mona Lisa look as though she is realistically emerging from the surface of the painting. The soft atmosphere surrounding her makes it seem as if her expression could change at any second.

Leonardo's religious paintings often have fantastic backgrounds with rocks and winding rivers, which suggest that the figures are not of this world. Here he gave Mona Lisa the same kind of backdrop. Folds in her sleeves and the twisting scarf over her shoulder resemble the cascading topography behind her, linking her more closely to it. The stone spires and pinnacles of the background do not represent a real place but were created by Leonardo's imagination.

Mona Lisa was married to a rich silk merchant, Francesco di Bartolomeo di Zanobi del Giocondo. In Italy, the painting is called *La Gioconda*, taking its title from the woman's married name, but in English-speaking countries it is known as the *Mona Lisa*, an adaptation of her title, Madonna, and first name, Lisa. Little is known about her, though according to Vasari's romantic report, to keep her from becoming gloomy while he painted, the artist ordered musicians and jesters to amuse her.

Leonardo worked on this picture for years, adding thin layers of paint to achieve the subtle effects of light and shadow, which have now darkened. After the artist's death, the *Mona Lisa* was purchased by the king of France, and now it is in the Louvre.

The Virgin and Child with Saint Anne

In this painting, Leonardo returned to the theme that he had explored in his cartoon. Here Saint Anne, Mary, and Jesus appear with a lamb instead of the Baptist. At the top is Saint Anne, who looks at her daughter tenderly, with pride. Mary sits on her lap as she reaches over for her son, who plays with a lamb. Jesus responds with a questioning glance to his mother, who is the center of attention. Monumental, but human as no Mary ever had been in art before, she is endowed with mighty limbs and a grand torso. The placement of the heads forms a gentle, sloping diagonal that links the grandmother, the mother, the child, and the lamb, unifying the composition.

Jesus Embraces the Lamb

One of the symbols of Christ's inevitable death is a lamb, because it was the animal that, though innocent, was traditionally sacrificed in religious ceremonies. Leonardo shows Jesus embracing the lamb, aware of his role on earth. Mary, protective of her son, restrains him.

The rocky and mist-filled landscape behind the figures is typical of Leonardo's works, but here the bluish distance seems farther away from the foreground than before. The water and mountains seem to dissolve into the sky, creating an otherworldly setting for the holy figures.

Leonardo had made careful studies of the Apennines, the mountain range that runs the length of Italy, to explore the appearance of mountains in the distance. He used what he learned as well as his imagination in creating the hazy background of *The Virgin and Child with Saint Anne*.

Leonardo was in Milan in the service of the new French rulers when he painted this work. It was possibly commissioned by the king of France, Louis XII. The subject was of great interest to Leonardo, and he always had difficulty finishing the things that he cared about the most. The largest unfinished area is the cloak over Mary's legs, which seems flat. Additional layers of thin paint would have added texture and shadows to the fabric.

Saint John the Baptist

In one of his last paintings, Leonardo created this mysterious image of Saint John the Baptist in his role as the prophet who predicted the coming of the Messiah. Instead of the fiery preacher, Leonardo shows him making silent, personal contact with the viewer. Saint John lived alone in the desert, far from worldly pleasures, to find a purely spiritual life. Verrocchio, in *The Baptism of Christ,* showed the saint's bony frame clothed in the traditional camel's hair shirt, but Leonardo gave his saint a soft body and a smooth face that seems free from hardship in the desert sun. The reed cross is the Baptist's only traditional attribute.

Emerging from the darkness that encircles him, the Baptist addresses us directly as he gently smiles and elegantly swings his right hand across his body to point upward. With his left hand, he gestures toward himself. The pantomime conveys his message to us: "Listen to me, the Messiah is coming." This beautiful pointing gesture can also be found in *The Virgin and Saint Anne* cartoon as well as in *The Last Supper* and *The Adoration of the Magi.* The characters that use it direct our attention to heaven. Here the pointing gesture is the main feature of the work. Leonardo also makes the *sfumato* effect more extreme than ever before. Even though the picture has darkened over time, we still see the saint dramatically emerging from the dark, smoky atmosphere to convey his message to us.

Further political problems in Milan caused Leonardo to leave the city in 1512 and spend some time in the countryside. There he created a

THE VIRGIN AND CHILD WITH SAINTS ANNE
AND JOHN THE BAPTIST (DETAIL)

magnificent group of drawings, later dubbed the "Deluges," in which he explored the movement of water. Leonardo showed water in swirling, turbulent motion, overtaking the earth like disastrous tidal waves. Even without depicting people, Leonardo could use light, shade, and motion to create a natural as well as fantastic scene filled with emotion.

Leonardo's next patron was Giuliano de' Medici of the great Florentine Medici family, whose brother became Pope Leo X in 1513. The artist took residence in the Vatican Palace in Rome, where another great artist, Raphael, was creating his splendid decorations in the papal apartments. After Giuliano's death, Leonardo was invited by the king of France, Francis I, to live and work in the comfortable, small château of Cloux, near the king's residence in northwestern France. The king, according to the report of Benvenuto Cellini, a sculptor in his employ, "did not believe that a man had been born who knew as much as Leonardo, not only in the spheres of painting, sculpture, and architecture, but also that he was a very great philosopher." Leonardo spent his last days there, until his death in 1519. Vasari reported that he died with the king by his side. He also wrote, "All who had known Leonardo were grieved beyond words by their loss, for no one had ever shed such luster on the art of painting."

A DELUGE

In A Deluge, *Leonardo observed how nature's forces can be destructive and violent. In* Studies for a Nativity, *he experimented with gestures and poses to express a tender scene of the Madonna and Child.*

STUDIES FOR A NATIVITY

What Makes a Leonardo

This is a second version of *The Virgin of the Rocks*, painted by Leonardo and his assistants. Leonardo explored the same themes again and again.

Through painting and drawing,
Leonardo explored the variety of nature.

Leonardo used deep shadows to make things look three-dimensional. He did not use outlines.

The gestures and expressions of Leonardo's figures convey real-life emotions.

He often used aerial, or atmospheric, perspective, the technique of making the background look blurry and pale to make it seem far away.